You will find your way

POETRY & MUSINGS

You Will Find Your Way is a work of creative non-fiction. The collection of poems and musings contained within this book are not about a singular person, relationship, event, or experience. The writings are thematic in nature, inspired by varied individual and collective experiences, conversations and reflections spanning through childhood, young adulthood, and adulthood.

Copyright © Naomi Arnold 2024.

All rights reserved. Content from this book must not be reproduced, distributed or transmitted in any form or by any means without the prior written permission of the author, with the exception of brief quotations embedded in reviews or other non-commercial uses permitted by Australian copyright law.

The content within the book expresses the lived experience and personal views of the author. Any views, reflections or advice contained herein may not be suitable for your individual context. Consult with the relevant professional where appropriate.

Naomi Arnold (Author & Cover Illustrator)
www.naomiarnold.com

Illustrations by Nicola Newman:
www.nicolanewman.com

ISBN (paperback): 978-1-7635708-0-1
ISBN (e-book): 978-1-7635708-1-8

You will find your way

POETRY & MUSINGS

Naomi Arnold

Content Warning

Abuse, depression, anxiety and grief

If you feel you need immediate support,
please call the relevant support services in your
country (e.g., in Australia, you can call
the Beyond Blue Support Service on
1300 22 4636).

Acknowledgment

To the friends
who got me through
- you know who you are -
thank you and I love you.

Dedication

This collection of writing
is for those who have survived
the arc of a toxic relationship,
the sting of an incomprehensible betrayal,
or the loss of hope in humanity.

May you trust yourself
and your experience.
May you heal.
May you move forward.
May you live a life free of the grasp
of those people who have harmed you.

Here's to a future,
where you are
free to be you.

Preface

I do not recall learning how to write poems. Some might say that I am not a poet. Others might argue that I am clearly an amateur. These statements *might* be true.

What I know *is* true, is that this collection of poems flowed out of me. I would be going about my day, and one would land on my consciousness, abruptly compelling me to stop what I was doing to write it down.

It seemed selfish to keep these musings to myself. Surely, I am not the only one who these words might sing to? Maybe sharing them would help me, and others, feel less alone?

If this collection of writings speak to you, I am sorry that you can relate to the experiences expressed within them. I know of the hurt you have felt. I know of the grief you have experienced.

I also know that it is possible to heal, to move forward, and to live a life free of the grasp of those people who have harmed you.

I sincerely hope that a future where you are free to safely be you is not far away.

Naomi

Contents

Endings **1**
Rescind the Contract 3
The Caretaker 4
The Hierarchy 6
Me and Mine 10
The Steps You Took 12
Internal Gardens 14
Leave 15
When Did You Know? 16
Before and After 18

Denial **21**
Behind Closed Doors 23
The Vine 24
Benefit of the Doubt 25
Wasted Investment 26
Please Let It Be A Dream 27
Reading Glasses 28
When Your World Tilts 30
The Scientist, The Friend 31
Tell Someone 33

Anger 35
I'm Angry..................... 37
Eruption...................... 38
An Inspired idea............. 39
Patriarchal Institution...... 40
The Myth of the Consequence.... 41
Two Faces..................... 42
Fan the Flames................ 43
Control....................... 44
You Have Changed!............. 47

Bargaining................ 49
Hypervigilance................ 51
Over-......................... 52
Empathy Isn't Magic........... 54
The Moving Line............... 56
Responsibility................ 57
Recast the Narrative.......... 58
Empty Promises................ 60
Dialogue...................... 61
It Happens in Threes.......... 63

Depression................. 65
The Crying.................... 67
The Ability to Dream.......... 69
Burnout....................... 70
Mirrored Mask................. 72

Values Entrapment......................	73
Busy...	75
Imprint...	77
Deserved Better...........................	78
Friends are Family......................	79
Acceptance...........................	**81**
Lonely...	83
Like the Rain...............................	84
Dormant.......................................	85
Nature...	86
Wildflowers..................................	87
Empty House................................	88
You Will Find Your Way..............	89
Spaces...	90
Desirable......................................	91
Beginnings...........................	**93**
Beach Walk...................................	95
Blossom..	96
Retiring the Mask........................	97
Possibilities are Blossoming........	98
I Can Dream Again......................	99
New Year's Eve.............................	103
My 40th Year................................	104
Inner Harmony............................	106
Live Your Life..............................	107

Endings

Demise. Finale. Exit. Release.

NAOMI ARNOLD

Rescind the Contract

I realised today,
as my heart pounded,
my belly twisted and turned,
and my anxiety peaked,
that the reason I was here,
the reason I was always here,
was because long ago,
I had unknowingly signed
an inner contract within
the depths of my mind.
A promise to myself
around what I should do,
how I should be,
and who I must value.
It is time,
and I have the power,
to rescind that inner contract,
to let myself free,
to do as I choose,
to be who I want to be.

YOU WILL FIND YOUR WAY

The Caretaker

For so long,
> my identity has been wrapped up
> in the role of The Caretaker.

For so long,
> I've tried to be:
> generous,
> thoughtful,
> understanding.

For so long,
> I've treaded carefully,
> not wanting to hurt feelings.

For so long,
> I've trained my face
> to not form shapes
> that might cause alarm.

For so long,
> I've been quiet,
> careful to not disrupt
> the fragile egos around me.

NAOMI ARNOLD

Not today.

Today,
I anchor myself in the knowing that
    my usefulness,
    my helpfulness,
    my caregiving,
    is not tangled up with my worthiness.

Today,
    I speak up.
    I let my face be free.
    I tread as loudly as I need.
    I turn that generosity,
    that thoughtfulness,
    that understanding,
    toward me.

You have lost The Caretaker.
She is now free.

YOU WILL FIND YOUR WAY

The Hierarchy

The lens through which
you see the world
is so coloured
by your warped understanding
of the concept of 'respect'.

You won't say it out loud
or outside of your family,
but there is a hierarchy.

There is a secret,
never overtly stated,
but well-known order,
concerning who
must obey whom.

Naturally,
you're at the top
of this hierarchy.
You must be respected,
at all costs.

So quick to demand it
with such intensity,
whilst refusing
with equal force
to give it in return.

Because quietly,
others are
below you.

Not as intelligent.
Not as experienced.
Not as intuitive.
Not as logical.
Not as wise.

And I have now committed
the ultimate sin -
stating this hierarchy exists,
calling it into question.

The punishment
for my crime
is already in motion.

YOU WILL FIND YOUR WAY

You push me down
your self-built
ladder.

I'm meant
to fear,
to dread,
my descent
down,
down,
down
the hierarchy.

But I'm no longer afraid.

I simply step off the ladder,
landing on sturdy feet,
I walk away.

You don't need to respect me.
I need to respect me.
And I do.

NAOMI ARNOLD

YOU WILL FIND YOUR WAY

Me and Mine

I figured you out
a long time ago.
I learned how to be,
how to not rock the boat.

I knew to show interest,
to pretend to need counsel,
to ask the right questions,
and to ignore the insults.

I learned to sense trouble,
I knew when to deflect,
how to change the topic,
and what made you upset.

I knew what puffed you up,
what made you feel good,
what to do for you to like me,
and where we really stood.

It would have continued this way
if you'd kept targeting me.
I told myself it was worth it because
I love you and I'd learned how to be.

But then your sights turned
and you focused on them.
They don't know what I know.
They don't know how to stay safe,
how to heal from your sting.

My job is to protect them
from people like you,
and in that moment I knew
exactly what to do.

It was finally time
to put me and mine first.

So I say goodbye
with a heavy heart.
I will always love you,
but now from afar.

YOU WILL FIND YOUR WAY

The Steps You Took

When you hurt me
with your actions and words,
you would focus on the event,
like it happened in isolation
and how you thought it was deserved.

But the part I can't get past
is the number of choices you made,
the number of steps you took,
that led to your behaviour,
that led to those words,
that led to you following through,
that led to you not stopping yourself,
that led to you not seeking help.

Then even after the event,
you continue to make choices,
you continue to enact steps,
to not take responsibility,
to not apologise,
to not show humility,

to twist the story,
to spread the lies,
to justify your actions and words,
to pretend you're the victim,
to paint me as the villain,
to still not seek help.

I think about how exhausting that must be,
to make all those choices,
to take all those steps,
to do the mental gymnastics,
to fight off the inner truth-teller,
to pretend it was an isolated event,
to keep up the facade,
to convince yourself you're not like *them*.

Part of me has compassion for you
and the suffering this must bring,
but then I remember:
the number of choices you've made,
the number of steps you've taken,
to commit to being this way.

YOU WILL FIND YOUR WAY

Internal Gardens

You have spent your lifetime
tending to the internal gardens of others.

You have consistently offered:
    protection,
    light,
    energy,
    sustenance,
    devotion.

It is time to entrust them with
tending to their own internal gardens.

It is time to offer yourself:
    protection,
    light,
    energy,
    sustenance,
    devotion.

It is time to wholeheartedly focus on
tending to your own internal garden.

Leave

Stop waiting for
the perfect time to leave.

No such time exists.

And for this reason every moment
is the perfect time to leave.

Trust yourself.
Take a step now.

Know the unknowns will become known.
Know you will have your back.

Choose this moment to leave.

YOU WILL FIND YOUR WAY

When Did You Know?

My mentor once reminded me
that if I trusted my intuition,
there was a moment where I could see
that I would end up in this position.

When I look back with hindsight
there was always at least one red flag,
a moment where something didn't sit right,
where I dismissed myself for being a hag.

But now this person has hurt me
more times than I can count,
and I simply cannot unsee
those red flags I can no longer discount.

So my mentor simply asked me
"When did you know?"
because this might help me see
where I could grow.

Next time I will be able to believe
that when I mysteriously know,
it is definitely time to leave
before my life becomes a drama show.

*Note: This poem was inspired by Lena West
who once asked me "When did you know?"*

YOU WILL FIND YOUR WAY

Before and After

In the quiet,
before the traumatic event,
you think your life
is in order.

You are naive.
You are hopeful.
You are tenacious.

The blow hits hard.
Your life explodes.

You stand looking
at the shattered pieces
all around you.

You wonder how
you did not see
the explosion coming?

NAOMI ARNOLD

In the quiet,
after the traumatic event,
you know your life
was never in order.

You are wounded.
You are cautious.
You are strong.

There is a clear line
between the
before and after.

You pick up the
shattered pieces.

You must go on.

Denial

Betrayal. Shock. Confusion. Self-doubt.

Behind Closed Doors

You watch them put on the mask each day.
You see how much they are adored.
You listen to people sing their praise.
If only they knew what you had endured.

You watch them take off their mask
when you are the only one who can see.
They privately treat you with contempt
and you think "perhaps it's just me?"

Each time behind closed doors,
you convince yourself to stay,
thinking perhaps the mask will stick
and they'll turn that charisma toward you someday.

YOU WILL FIND YOUR WAY

The Vine

Bending
    and twisting,

around your predefined structures,
following the rules for survival,
the guidelines for thriving.

Occasionally reaching
    out into
            the empty spaces,
      up tall
            in the sunlight,
   momentarily
      touching freedom.

But you always notice,
and swiftly take control,
wrapping me back around the structure,
back where you want me to be,
back to doing what I'm told.

NAOMI ARNOLD

Benefit of the Doubt

It has been a life mission of mine
of which I've been devout:
Actively searching for a sign
to give the benefit of the doubt.

Surely you didn't do it on purpose,
that incomprehensible awful thing.
Maybe you were just uncontrollably nervous,
when you said those words that sting.

You were probably doing the best you can
as you unfurled on me with passion.
Simply responding from past trauma,
maybe I should show more compassion.

So even though you continue to hurt me,
even though you lie to gain clout,
as you bury me in your emotional debris,
I'll continue to give you the benefit of the doubt.

YOU WILL FIND YOUR WAY

Wasted Investment

I keep fixating on the thought
of the time I have committed,
of how hard I have fought
and how much I have permitted.

Why would I leave now
when I have worked so hard,
when I have made a vow
to always remove the shard?

Will it have been a waste?
Could things possibly get better?
Is there a way to remove the distaste?
To continue to be our go-getter?

How bad do things have to get
before I stop fixating on a wasted investment,
and instead show myself some respect
and prioritise my own contentment?

Please Let It Be A Dream

My wish is to be Zhuangzi's butterfly
          dreaming about this human life,
   casting stories for drama and interest,
          while I sleep peacefully at night.

YOU WILL FIND YOUR WAY

Reading Glasses

I remember the first time I got reading glasses.
I was bewildered and astonished.
Had I really not been seeing clearly for so long?
Had I really been overcompensating,
straining so much
it triggered migraines and fatigue?

I remember the first time I got reading glasses.
The discomfort of the adjustment period.
The noticing of something different,
something that didn't sit quite right,
as I went through the process
of wearing them in.

I remember the first time I got reading glasses.
It feels like that moment now.

I've been given the new glasses.
I have the correct lens.
I see who you are
and how you operate.

I recognise the straining when I'm with you,
the later experience of migraines and fatigue.
I feel the discomfort in knowing this.
I recognise the adjustment period.

I remember the first time I got reading glasses.
I try to take them off.
I need a break from the change,
the strangeness of it.

But this only makes it worse.
Once I could see, I could not unsee.
Once I knew, I knew.
Everything was so clear.

I remember the first time I got reading glasses.
And how with each
    minute,
    hour,
    day,
I adjusted.

Life got easier and I shall
no longer go without.

YOU WILL FIND YOUR WAY

When Your World Tilts

Your world suddenly tilts.
The ground shifts under your feet.
Nothing is as it was before.

You try every trick you can
to make the world tilt back.

You shift your weight to one side,
and then to the other.
You lean a little forward,
then you lean a little backward.
You jump up and down,
you try standing perfectly still.

But you know,
there is nothing you can do.

This is the way the world is now.
You must start anew.

NAOMI ARNOLD

The Scientist, The Friend

You suspect it is there:
The microscopic germ
that he uses to weaken you,
unidentified in the petri dish,
denied the opportunity to be examined
through a microscope.

The Scientist tells you:
The germ does not exist,
it lives only in your mind.
And who are you to question him,
for he is The Scientist.

Then one day,
following a reluctant confession
you make to The Friend,
she brings a microscope.

The Friend examines,
the petri dish.

YOU WILL FIND YOUR WAY

She exclaims with alarm:
the germ is indeed here,
the germ is thriving,
the germ is being used,
to weaken you.
The Scientist deceives you.
Let me help you.

You escape
The Scientist,
hand in hand
with your rescuer,
The Friend.

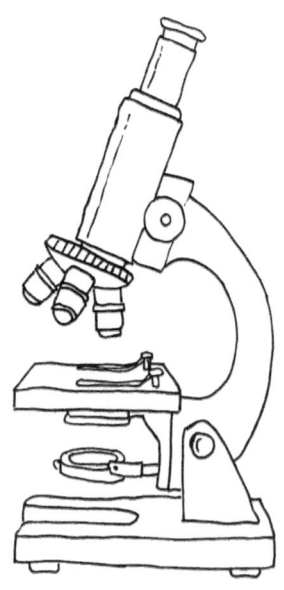

NAOMI ARNOLD

Tell Someone

Abuse thrives in secrecy.
It breeds denial.

Her healing began
when she told someone,
when she showed someone,
when they boldly confirmed
what was happening
was indeed wrong.

The hold of the secret was broken.
The hold of denial was released.
Taking the first step toward freedom
finally felt possible.

Someone believed her.
Someone believed in her.
And now,
she believed in herself.

Anger

Realisation. Pain. Injustice. Eruption.

NAOMI ARNOLD

I'm Angry

I'm angry that
I've never been allowed
to be angry.
I'm angry that
I'm always expected
to be calm,
measured,
unemotional.
I'm angry that
no matter what you do,
what you say,
how harmful you are,
or how angry you get,
that this is okay.
Yet I'm not allowed
to be angry.
I'm angry,
and today,
you're just going to
have to live with that.

Eruption

The fire
    has been within me,
        my whole life,
            dormant
        and carefully managed.
    But now I feel it,
        rising to the surface,
            where it needs to be,
        released,
    escaping those tight confines,
flowing wild and free.

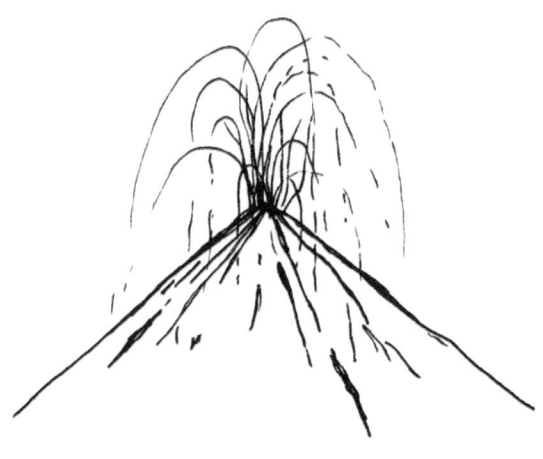

NAOMI ARNOLD

An Inspired Idea

When I shared an idea,
it was like you never heard,
quick to dismiss it,
so you could get in the last word.

When he later shared the same idea,
you would come with a straight face
to share this new inspired suggestion,
to teach something I must embrace.

If it had only happened once,
perhaps I'd think it was a mistake.
But now I see the unfortunate pattern,
and realise it's women that you hate.

YOU WILL FIND YOUR WAY

Patriarchal Institution

It's your fault that I don't feel safe anymore,
that I've lost all faith in men.
I was never like this before,
but I can't see myself trusting again.

You taught me that we only exist
to satisfy your ego and needs,
that our feelings will always be dismissed,
once you are done with your misdeeds.

I see how you support each other
in justifying your manipulation and abuse.
Whether a friend, lover, father or brother -
you always have an excuse.

I hope someday to meet and trust a man
who truly defies this patriarchal institution -
who is not pretending as part of the plan,
to continue his self-serving constitution.

NAOMI ARNOLD

The Myth of the Consequence

We get taught as children
that there are consequences
when you do the wrong thing.

We get taught that this is necessary,
an important lesson
that we should not question.

But now that I'm grown,
I know this isn't true.

I experience consequences
even when it is you who did wrong.
There are rarely consequences
for people who look like you.

The myth of the consequence
is one of the many weapons you use,
to keep your power,
to oppress,
to abuse.

YOU WILL FIND YOUR WAY

Two Faces

Beware of those who are masters
at portraying themselves
to the external world
as charismatic characters,
advocates for feminism,
and trusted heroes.

Beware of those who are masters
at saving who they truly are
for their private world,
emotionally immature,
manipulative and abusive,
self-serving villains.

Beware of those who are masters
at using these faces
to take away your power,
to entrap you in their game
of two faces.

Fan the Flames

Nothing further inflames
the ferociousness of your anger more
than simply holding up a mirror
for you to witness it in full force.

YOU WILL FIND YOUR WAY

Control

If you were honest with yourself
and somewhat self-aware,
you would admit:

> You wish I was still quiet,
> lacking confidence and self-worth,
> desperate to belong.

If you were honest with yourself
and somewhat self-aware,
you would admit:

> As I became more confident,
> independent, capable, and strong,
> you started to feel everything was wrong.

If you were honest with yourself
and somewhat self-aware,
you would admit:

The old me was easier to control.
This me didn't have boundaries.
This me was eager to please.
This me did what she was told.

If you were honest with yourself
and somewhat self-aware,
you would admit:

> You thrived on the attention you received,
> on your perceived superiority,
> on my co-dependency.

> You taught me that this was:
> the only way to be loved
> the only way to be respected
> the only way to be worthy.

If I'm honest with myself
and somewhat self-aware,
I can admit:

YOU WILL FIND YOUR WAY

> I believed you.
> I kept these patterns alive.
> I hoped some day
> you would love me the way I love you.

If I'm honest with myself
and somewhat self-aware,
I can admit:

> I deserve better.
> It is time to stop waiting,
> to start healing,
> to stand on my own.

You Have Changed!

"You have changed!"
is often flung as an insult.

I've always wanted
to ask in response:

"Why are you okay
with the fact
that you have you not?"

Bargaining

Powerless. Adrift. Negotiation. Bookends.

Hypervigilance

From the moment I wake up
to the second I fall asleep,
always on edge,
always quietly observing,
always adjusting accordingly.

Every word,
every facial expression,
every subtle shift in tone,
and every action,
monitored carefully.
Tiptoeing around,
making myself small,
nodding along
and never reacting.

The goal is to stay under the radar.
I'll be safe that way.
Safe from your wrath perhaps,
but not safe to be me,
not safe to be free.

YOU WILL FIND YOUR WAY

Over-

Do you ever
> over-explain
> in an attempt
> to be understood?

Do you ever
> overcompensate
> in an attempt
> to be viewed as fair?

Do you ever
> remind yourself
> that sometimes
> people choose to
> not understand you,
> in which case,
> over-explaining
> does not serve you?

Do you ever
    remind yourself
    that sometimes
    in your focus on being fair to others
    you forget to be fair to yourself?
    In which case,
    overcompensating
    does not serve you?

Do you ever
    acknowledge that you know
    over-explaining and overcompensating
    does not always serve you,
    but you decide to keep doing it anyway?
    It is part of who you are.
    You will always make every effort
    to be understood
    to be fair
    to sleep at night knowing you did your best.
    And this is how it serves you.

YOU WILL FIND YOUR WAY

Empathy Isn't Magic

You keep waiting,
convincing yourself that
    compassion,
    empathy,
    patience,
will offer a solution.

Eventually,
they will learn:
    to treat you well,
    to love you well,
    to see you.

But empathy isn't magic.
Compassion isn't magic.
Patience isn't magic.

You've waited long enough.
You've restitched
those wounds too many times.

All the empathy,
compassion,
patience in the world,
will not change this.

It is time for you to:
    see you,
    love you well,
    treat you well.

Turn that gift for extending
    patience,
    compassion,
    empathy,
toward you.

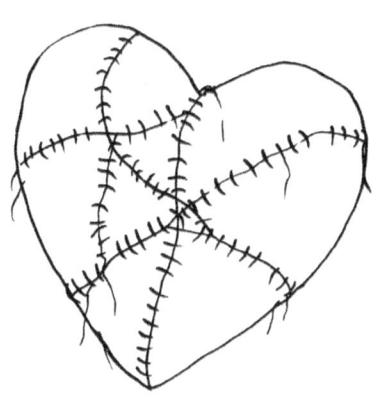

YOU WILL FIND YOUR WAY

The Moving Line

Each time they hurt me,
each time they cause pain,
I find a way to justify
why I should stay.

Deep down I question:
What do they have to do?
Where will I draw the line?
How much will I let them put me through?

At what point do I put a stop
to the never-ending moving line,
and say that is enough,
it's time to leave,
it's time to let myself shine?

Responsibility

I always took responsibility:
    for motivating you,
    for your healing,
    for your self-growth,
    for your health.

Each time you hurt me,
each time you lashed out,
    you would later promise to do better,
    ask me to help,
    beg me to stay.
So I would take responsibility yet again.

But I have finally realised
    your behaviour,
    your motivations,
    your healing,
    your self-growth,
    your health,
are your responsibility, not mine.

Only you can decide who you want to be.
I will no longer place that pressure on me.

YOU WILL FIND YOUR WAY

Recast the Narrative

When you cause harm,
when you do the wrong thing,
I hear the ring of an internal alarm,
a warning of your predictable next swing.

Rather than give a genuine apology,
you will choose to twist the truth,
you will manipulate psychology
and become a storytelling sleuth.

You will convince yourself and the family
that I was actually the aggressor,
that I overreacted and used profanity
to become the ultimate oppressor.

Rather than take responsibility
for the fact that it was you who hurled abuse,
you will lean in to your emotional immaturity
and oh what a story you will produce.

Rather than show any vulnerability
or offer genuine attempts to be collaborative,
because you are incapable of humility,
you will always choose to recast the narrative.

YOU WILL FIND YOUR WAY

Empty Promises

I wish I had a dollar
for every promise that you made.
It would outperform every investment
and oh how much I would have saved.

I wish I had a dollar
for each time you promised to do better.
My account would be abundant
and I'd have no financial pressure.

I wish I had a dollar
even that last time I heard you promise
that you'd never hurt me again
when I left with empty pockets.

Dialogue

I was taught,
    dialogue is critical
    to resolving conflict.

I was taught,
    I owed people
    no matter what they did to me
    an opportunity to dialogue.

I was taught,
    dialogue takes a long time,
    a lot of skill,
    much more than I possessed.

I was taught,
    to leave the moderation of dialogue
    to those who've mastered the skill.
    My role was to listen,
    to answer questions,
    to be respectful,
    and to never react.

YOU WILL FIND YOUR WAY

I was taught,
    if dialogue failed,
    it must have been my fault.
    I must not have done it properly,
    and more dialogue was required as a result.

I learned that,
    dialogue is a weapon
    that abusers like to use,
    to induce conversation,
    to hide the bruises they've issued.

I learned that,
    dialogue is about power
    and taking mine away,
    reinserting your authority
    and putting me in my place.

I learned that,
    this is not truly dialogue
    and it's okay to step away,
    that my safety is non-negotiable
    and to no longer give access
    to me in this way.

It Happens in Threes

When the life curveballs hit 1, 2, 3…
When you get knocked down 1, 2, 3…
When you are lost in the pain 1, 2, 3…

Remind yourself, you've been here before.
Oh yes you can, get back up once more.

You are resilient. You are strong.
You can recover when everything feels wrong.

When you force yourself to breathe 1, 2, 3…
When you struggle to your feet 1, 2, 3…
When you reach out for support 1, 2, 3…

Remind yourself, it takes time to heal.
And oh yes, it's important to feel.

Things will get better. You will see.
Just one step at time 1, 2, 3…

Depression

Sadness. Brokenness. Distrust. Emptiness.

NAOMI ARNOLD

The Crying

I have cried before,
but never like this.

I was possessed.
    The foetal position.
    The sobbing.
    The shaking.
    The hot tears.
    The hopelessness.

My body was exhausted.
    So heavy.
    So drained.
    Eyes, puffy.
    Nose, raw.

Surely soon the tears would break.

YOU WILL FIND YOUR WAY

As the waves finally begin to ease,
the mind takes their place.
> So inflamed.
> So hurt.
> Thoughts, busy.
> Feelings, bruised.

Surely soon this too would pass.

Then just like a cheeky hiccup,
the moment you thought the tears were gone,
they come back with heightened ferocity
and the cycle begins once more.

NAOMI ARNOLD

The Ability to Dream

I have always been a dreamer,
dreaming up big possibilities,
for me and for others.
Having a vision to grasp
brought me hope,
gave me purpose,
nudged me forward.

But then suddenly, one day,
I woke up and all my dreams were gone.
And worse, it would seem,
I could no longer dream.

I felt the precise moment when
the capability faded away from me.
I felt the ability to dream leave.
No hope, vision, purpose or possibility.

There was no grand gesture,
just a quiet slipping away.
Now it feels forever out of reach.

YOU WILL FIND YOUR WAY

Burnout

It sneaks up on you
- the fatigue -
bone tired,
you observe with intrigue.

You didn't notice the signs,
you didn't see it coming,
body and mind,
completely succumbing.

It weighs on you
- the heaviness -
you try to push through,
but it clings to the messiness.

You go about each day
with very little left to give.
You save your smiles for others
and silently think "this is no way to live".

You wonder what it feels like
to have boundless energy,
to go about each day
without being ruled by lethargy.

If you could just find a way
to rebuild your capacity,
maybe you could dream again,
oh, the audacity!

YOU WILL FIND YOUR WAY

Mirrored Mask

Did you ever
really love me?
Or did you love
seeing the reflection of yourself
in my mirrored mask?

Values Entrapment

I have come to the realisation
that my values
aren't really my values.
They are ideals shaped by socialisation.
Rules for how I should operate,
how I will be measured
as a decent human,
as someone worthy of love.

I have to come to the realisation
that those values you admire in me,
can be leveraged
manipulated,
and used to ensure I stay
where you want me to be.

I have come to the realisation
that loyalty,
means loyalty to you
and to those you approve,
not loyalty to me.

YOU WILL FIND YOUR WAY

That empathy and compassion
is to be directed at you
and to others,
never at me.

That integrity
means doing the right thing
by you and a chosen few,
but not by me.

I have come to the realisation
that I have been lured,
entrapped,
kept hostage,
by my supposed values.
They have been used as bait
to ensure I stay,
comply,
justify mistreatment,
sacrifice myself,
and never truly be seen.

Busy

Busy is my armour.
Busy is my defence.
Busy is my game plan.

I distract.
I evade.
I dodge.
I keep moving.

I'm determined
to not let it catch me -
the depression.

I feel it at my heels.
The second I slow down,
it pounces,
smothers me.
pulls me under.

YOU WILL FIND YOUR WAY

So through the exhaustion,
through the pain,
I keep moving,
I keep busy,
determined to
not let it catch me again.

Imprint

They wear you down.
They chip away at your spirit.
They mould you into their desired shape.
You feel beaten.

One day something shifts.
A quiet determination emerges.
You suddenly know:
No matter what move they make,
the imprint of your soul shall remain.

YOU WILL FIND YOUR WAY

Deserved Better

I feel sad for her,
the girl who did not know
that she deserved better,
for she stayed too long
and slowly lost her glow
each time I met her.

I could see the signs
of how they were doing her wrong,
but never knew what to say or do.
I feel sad for her,
the girl who felt she didn't belong,
because I'd once been there too.

I must find a way
to be brave upon our next visit
and safely let her know.
I want to be there for her,
the girl with the fading spirit,
and watch her spark regrow.

Friends are Family

When the waves of life pulled me under,
as I thrashed in the sea unable to breathe,
as the storm bellowed with endless thunder,
when I was convinced fate had me by the teeth.

I found a gift shining in the darkness,
the best gift one could ever receive,
a guiding light that I could harness
to break free and discover a reprieve.

The strength returned to my body and mind,
my soul refilled with hope, joy and possibility.
I promised to always return this gift in kind,
should the giftee's world wobble with instability.

Dear friend, that gift that revived my capacity,
was the realisation that friends are family.

Acceptance

Healing. Freedom. Possibility. Movement.

Lonely

I have lived
long enough to know
that sometimes you can be lonelier
in the company
of those who you are not well suited
than in the company
of yourself alone.

Like the Rain

Like the rain
    takes the heaviness out of the humidity,
    washes away the debris,
    smothers the fire and heat,
    soaks deep into the soil,
    heals the scorched earth,
    and regenerates all things green,
feel your heart heal
and this new season begin.

Dormant

Sometimes we are dormant:
    not visibly active,
    prioritising rest,
    conserving energy,
    building our root systems,
    replenishing strength,
    surviving adverse conditions.

Sometimes we are blooming:
    visibly active,
    vibrant,
    bright,
    loud,
    head held high,
    more obviously thriving.

Both are necessary.
Both are beautiful.

YOU WILL FIND YOUR WAY

Nature

In nature,
we find expressions
of what we cannot articulate
with human words.

NAOMI ARNOLD

Wildflowers

I aspire to be a wildflower,
    dancing tall and free,
not caring what people think,
not minding if they're called a weed,
        free,
        free,
        free as can be.

YOU WILL FIND YOUR WAY

Empty House

As I sit in this empty house
in the ashes of my past life
with everything that mattered
crumbling around me,
I notice something unexpected:
I feel lighter and freer
than I have ever felt before.

You Will Find Your Way

No matter what life curveballs are thrown,
no matter how bad your day:
You have the power, brilliance and support
to find your way.

No matter the abuse or toxicity,
no matter what the hell they say:
You have the knowing, strength and resourcefulness
to find your way.

No matter how much your nervous system shakes,
no matter how deep the dismay:
You have the tools, self-trust and stillness
to find your way.

No matter how much you feel the hurt,
no matter how much they betray:
You have the hope, love and vision
to find your way.

YOU WILL FIND YOUR WAY

Spaces

I'm meant to feel guilty
for no longer having space for you
in my heart.
I'm meant to feel shame
for no longer having space for you
in my life.

I'm meant to always hold space for you
to come and go as you choose.

But in the emptiness I realised that
those spaces were in fact wounds.
In your absence,
they began to breathe,
they began to heal,
they began to transform.

I've since reclaimed those spaces.
The are filled with love.
They are filled with joy.
They are filled with inner harmony.
They are empty no more.

Desirable

As I become less desirable to those who
create the rules for what is deemed desirable,
I feel more freedom to be who I want to be,
to let go of expectations and just be me.

Beginnings

Dawn. Genesis. Emergence. Rise

Beach Walk

Goodbye,
    blue horizon
    where the sea meets the sky,
    under the scorching sun
    where my dreams went to die.

Hello,
    toes grounded
    in the gritty sand below,
    a steady heartbeat resounded
    where new beginnings start to glow.

Blossom

You are allowed
    to blossom
where it is
    unexpected.

Retiring the Mask

I awoke early one summer morning
and realised my life felt anew.
I was not weighed down by mourning,
I no longer had to worry about you.

I could discard the hypervigilance,
I didn't have to gauge your mood.
There was not a hint of ambivalence,
nor concern for how I was viewed.

I could examine what I needed,
I could embrace just being me.
I felt I had finally succeeded,
at allowing myself to be free.

I had achieved the most challenging task:
That is, I had finally retired the mask.

YOU WILL FIND YOUR WAY

Possibilities are Blossoming

I was painting elegant wildflowers,
    dancing on the page in all shapes and sizes,
        splashes of soft watercolour,
      transforming shapes and lines.

I was painting elegant wildflowers,
    captivated by their beauty and strength,
    resonating with their imperfections,
    when a smile spread across my face.

I was painting elegant wildflowers,
      when my heart started to sing.
      The tune it was joyfully humming?
      "Possibilities are blossoming".

I Can Dream Again

It was disturbing,
the day I lost my ability to dream.
Without warning,
it quietly faded away,
no trail to be seen.

I know why it left me
alone in my grief -
what offended it's sensibilities,
so much that it had to leave.

The day I noticed it's fading light,
I had nothing in me,
not an ounce,
to compel it to stay,
to continue to fight.

So I must confess,
I let it slip away,
without a word
quietly into the night.

YOU WILL FIND YOUR WAY

I grieved for the loss,
the moment it left me.
Being a dreamer had been
so much a part of my identity.

But that grief swam around
with all the others,
so intertwined,
deep in my busy mind.

I went about my life,
one day at a time,
foundation by foundation,
rebuilding,
strengthening,
reconnecting with who I am,
and what I need to survive.

Then I realised in the solitude,
in the quiet moments,
my long lost dreamer
started softly whispering.

Subtle at first
with tentative,
quiet,
gentle
bursts.

But then louder
with big,
broad,
vibrant
strokes.

Larger,
bolder,
more audacious
than ever before.

In our solitude,
our time spent apart,
we'd rebuilt our confidence,
discarded the doubt,
reignited the spark.

YOU WILL FIND YOUR WAY

In that moment,
and I remember exactly when,
I knew with certainty
and to my relief:
I can dream again.

NAOMI ARNOLD

New Year's Eve

The whisper of a promise
that New Year's Eve can bring:
The idea that a shift is upon us,
as our hearts begin to sing.

It whispers that it is possible
to let go of all the pain.
No line feels uncrossable,
we start to dream again.

It whispers that we have the capability
to achieve our wildest goals.
It opens up the possibility
that we can heal our souls.

It whispers to be honest
about what we truly desire:
That it will grant our wish as promised,
so why not dream even higher?

The whisper of a promise
that New Year's Eve can bring:
The idea that a shift is upon us,
as our hearts begin to sing.

My 40th Year

In my youth,
>I used to always think,
>that by the time I was 20,
>I would be free,
>free to be who I want to be.

In my youth,
>I used to always think,
>that by the time I was 30,
>I'd be kicking goals,
>doing work helping other souls.

In my youth,
>I used to always think,
>that by the time I was 40,
>I would have found my flow,
>living life nice and slow.

As I enter my 40th year,
I thank younger me.

You had been both right and wrong.
You proved to be resilient and strong.
Your vision holds me in this next chapter:
    Living life nice and slow,
    pursuing new goals,
    finally free,
    to be who I want to be.

Inner Harmony

I awake each day
with a smile on my heart,
a face freely grinning,
embracing this new beginning.

I'm living where I want to be,
I'm surrounded by those who love me.
I no longer need to wear a mask,
being myself is all they ask.

My goal was to find inner harmony,
I now know it was always there inside of me.
It just needed a safe place
to truly thrive and take up space.

Live Your Life

You learned so much
in that prior life chapter.
You proved you are strong
and a capable adapter.
Go live your life,
be present and free.
The best is still to come,
you will see.

Nature told me a secret

Please enjoy this bonus chapter containing a sample of poems from Naomi's nature-inspired poetry collection, *Nature Told Me A Secret*.

NAOMI ARNOLD

Outside Noise

I hike within the bushland,
eyes captivated by trees and sky,
a sense of relief only nature offers,
my stresses wave goodbye.

But even in the bush so deep,
I see the impact of humankind,
I hear the noise of the outside world,
thoughts begin to invade my mind.

Traffic purrs from a distant road,
abandoned litter leaves its mark,
regular planes fly overhead,
odd profanity carved into bark.

I feel a sense of awe and wonder
when nature demonstrates the possibility,
one can coexist with undesired interruptions,
whilst being rooted deeply in tranquility.

YOU WILL FIND YOUR WAY

Whirlwind

I watched a whirlwind today.
        It swirled and twirled,
it didn't discriminate,
        picking up leaves,
    small branches and debris.

        Then as it dissipated,
    I watched a piece of litter
fluttering and dancing,
    dipping and diving
across the sky like a bird
        amongst the raining leaves.

I realised in that moment
        I have been in a whirlwind.
    Life circumstances
spinning me around and around,
    taking complete control of my body,
throwing me in every direction.

And only now,
as these circumstances dissipate,
do I feel like that piece of litter
fluttering around aimlessly,
knowing I will eventually find the earth,
I will eventually feel grounded again.

But for now,
I give in,
release my need for control,
and let the wind take me.

YOU WILL FIND YOUR WAY

Tonight

Tonight,
> I walk outside,
> look up at the sky,
> put a hand on my heart,
> release a breath with a sigh.

Tonight,
> you're on my mind,
> all you've been through,
> how lucky I am
> to have someone like you.

Tonight,
> I call to the moon,
> willing with all my might
> that things will get easier
> when you awake from this night.

Tonight,
> I quietly make a wish
> for only the stars to hear -
> may they share their blessings
> with you this year.

Tomorrow,
> when the new day breaks
> and you rise with the sun,
> I hope you feel a sense
> that a new chapter has begun.

Deciduous

Today,
I drop my leaves,
shake away the insecurities,
strengthen my foundations,
stripped bare to the core of me.

Tomorrow,
I reveal all my colours and form,
stand confident within myself,
head held high,
blooming for the world to see.

NAOMI ARNOLD

New Path

I look toward the new path,
it winds below the trees,
a track I am yet to follow,
the unknown causes unease.

I feel my heart rate quicken,
my mind begins to race,
intuition pulls me forward,
but hesitation slows my pace.

I glance toward the old path,
I know it inside out,
the ups, downs, twists, and turns,
a destination that causes doubt.

I feel my heart rate quicken,
my mind begins to race,
intuition pulls me forward,
determination quickens my pace.

Naomi hopes you enjoyed this free sample of poetry from *Nature Told Me A Secret*.

A moving collection of nature-inspired poetry for readers seeking healing, connection, and authentic self-discovery.

In this engaging and relatable anthology, Australian poet Naomi Arnold (they/she) offers reflections on what nature can teach us about resilience, growth, healing, and authentic self.

Through gentle and grounded verse spanning each season of the year, Naomi shows readers that it is possible to reclaim their power, embrace rhythms that work for them, awaken a quiet confidence, and rediscover their authentic self.

PRAISE FROM READERS

"Sweet little book... The poetry really makes you think about life."

"Poems that soothe your soul and provide solace."

"A great collection of beautiful and relatable poems."

AVAILABLE NOW
https://www.naomiarnold.com/books.

An Ask

Did you enjoy reading *You Will Find Your Way*?

If so, please consider supporting Naomi by taking a moment to leave a review on Amazon and / or Goodreads.

If you share an image of this book on social media, feel free to use the hashtag **#YouWillFindYourWay** so Naomi can follow along and connect with you.

Would you like to read more work by Naomi?

If so, you can find Naomi's other books via the following link or QR code:
https://www.naomiarnold.com/books.

Gentle Reminder

If you feel the content of this book has stirred up any big feelings and you need some support working through them, please reach out to the relevant support service in your country and/or the appropriate professional. In Australia, for example, you can start by calling Beyond Blue Support Service on 1300 22 4636.

newsletter

Sign up to Naomi's newsletter to be the first to receive book updates, excerpts and news: https://www.naomiarnold.com/subscribe.

About the author

Naomi Arnold (she/they) is a writer, researcher, award-winning life and business coach, and home educator. Naomi lives on the stolen land of the Yugambeh people in South East Queensland with their daughter and cheeky Cavoodle.

Naomi has a Master of Human Rights with Distinction, a Bachelor of Psychology with Honours, and a certified life coaching qualification. Naomi likes to draw on these topics in their writing, as well as her experience as an Autistic person with dynamic chronic illness.

Naomi's poetry collections include *You Will Find Your Way*, a powerful collection of poetry for readers seeking comfort and inspiration after a toxic relationship. Her latest poetry book, *Nature Told Me A Secret*, explores the lessons nature can offer on one's healing journey if we truly listen. Readers have described Naomi's work as "strong, brutal and fearless", "deep and relatable", "raw and resonant", "unapologetic, engaging and inspiring", and "relatable, healing and hope-inspiring."

**Learn more about Naomi via:
www.naomiarnold.com.**

www.ingramcontent.com/pod-product-compliance
Lightning Source LLC
Chambersburg PA
CBHW060613080526
44585CB00013B/814